Arnold Robinson has been a dec  and in that time, has cycled in every cc each region of Scotland, in Ireland and i South Yorkshire in 1935 and during the s many hundreds of miles in the county. He in this guide, some of them on many occasiuns.

After spending most of his childhood in Derbyshire and Nottinghamshire, in 1939 he moved to Sheffield to join the Police Force. When he retired in 1969, he held the rank of Detective Chief Superintendent and was head of the Criminal Investigation Department of Sheffield and Rotherham. After a spell as Police Consultant to Yorkshire Television and in industrial security, he became a freelance writer, broadcaster and photographer on outdoor activities, primarily cycling.

He regularly contributes articles and photographs to cycling magazines and was the author of a series of regional cycling guides covering the whole of Britain. He was also a major contributor of routes for *Cyclists' Britain* published in 1985 by Ordnance Survey/Pan Books.

His first of nearly two hundred broadcasts was made in 1939. For five years he was the presenter of BBC Radio Sheffield's cycling programme *On Your Bike.*

In recent years he has devoted his time increasingly to writing cycling route guides, a list of which is given at the back of this book.

Overleaf:

(Top) A steam pumping engine at the Elsecar Heritage Centre (Ride 6)

(Bottom) The Needle's Eye Folly on the Wentworth Woodhouse Estate (Ride 6)

be on for approximately a anticipated cycle for sixty years. had been in the field pumping beyond England and Wales. are the earliest in Europe. the first order in to subterranean reservoirs of water. to the north-east of the area.

CYCLING
around
SOUTH YORKSHIRE

Arnold Robinson

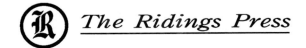

The Ridings Press

The fine view from the bridleway alongside the Broomhead Reservoir (Ride 4)

Photo credits:
Simon Laffoley 43, 47.
Arnold Robinson half title, 4, 11, 15 (top), 18, 19, 23, 51, 63, 67.
Duncan Smith frontispiece, 2, 15 (bottom), 27, 35, 55, 58, 59.

First published in 1996 by
The Ridings Press, 62 Sheldon Road, Sheffield, South Yorkshire S7 1GX

ISBN 0 9527235 0 6

© Arnold Robinson 1996

Typeset by Commercial Services
Carnson House, 1 Moorgate Road, Rotherham S60 2EE
Printed and bound in Doncaster

Contents

Introduction 6
Advice Before Setting Out.. 7

RIDES IN THE SHEFFIELD AREA

1. *"Bluebells, Crucibles and a Norman Abbey"*
   Millhouses - Whirlow - Dore - Bradway - Beauchief – 10 miles........................ 9

2. *"Waterwheels, Reservoirs and a Glimpse of the Moors"*
   Hunters Bar - Fulwood - Redmires - Rivelin - Crosspool – 14½ miles............. 13

3. *"Rivers, Reservoirs and Robin Hood"*
   Malin Bridge - Loxley - Bradfield - Strines - Dungworth – 19 miles 17

4. *"Wooded Ravines, Ancient Villages and a Bodysnatcher's Watch House"*
   Wharncliffe Side - Ewden - Midhope - Bradfield - Oughtibridge – 21½ miles .. 21

RIDES IN THE BARNSLEY AREA

5. *"A Flour Mill, a Disused Railway and a Folly Castle"*
   Worsbrough - Silkstone - Penistone - Wortley - Hood Green – 21½ miles 25

6. *"Steep Climbs, Steam Engines and some Delightful Villages"*
   Worsbrough - Wortley - Tankersley - Wentworth - Elsecar – 24 miles............. 29

7. *"Quiet Country Lanes, Peaceful Villages and a Country House"*
   Barnsley - Dodworth - Silkstone - Gunthwaite - Cawthorne – 19 miles............ 33

RIDES IN THE ROTHERHAM AREA

8. *"Ruins, Sword Dancers and an Elizabethan Hall"*
   Grange Park - Wentworth - Tankersley - Wortley - Grenoside – 19 miles 37

9. *"A Tudor Hall, a Canal and a Ride Through the Park"*
   Woodhouse - N. & S. Anston - Thorpe Salvin - Kiveton Park - Rother
   Valley – 19½ miles.. 41

10. *"Sleepy Villages, a Beautiful Abbey and a Mighty Spire"*
    Whiston - Thurcroft - Firbeck - Dinnington - Laughton – 28 miles 45

11. *"A Country Park, Ivanhoe's Castle and the Earth Centre"*
    Thrybergh - Denaby - Conisbrough - Tickhill - Braithwell – 25 miles 49

RIDES IN THE DONCASTER AREA

12. *"A Canal, Two Castles and a Nature Reserve"*
    Sprotborough - Mexborough - Conisbrough - Tickhill - Wadworth – 25½ miles   53

13. *"A Handful of Country Houses and a Murderous Cat!"*
    Cusworth - Sprotborough - Barnburgh - Hickleton - Brodsworth – 16½ miles .   57

14. *"Quiet Byroads and Forgotten Villages"*
    Bentley - Owston - Askern - Haywood - Arksey – 25 miles............................. 61

15. *"A River, Two Canals and a Ride Across the Flatlands"*
    Bentley - Barnby Dun - Sykehouse - Fishlake - Thorne – 26½ miles 65

Other Cycling Guides by Arnold Robinson.. 68

Introduction

Although a large part of South Yorkshire is industrialised and densely populated, it should not be forgotten that the region also offers a vast rural area of moorland, woods, farmland and open countryside which is criss-crossed by quiet, little-used byroads. This 'hidden' and unfrequented land is ideal for leisurely cycling where little motor traffic will be encountered. Once the built-up areas and main roads are left behind, the numerous country byroads and bridleways transport the cyclist into a different world of delightful vistas, interesting buildings and picturesque villages.

South Yorkshire offers an enviable selection of cycle routes with varying gradients suitable for all ages. Cycling enthusiasts and members of local clubs may want to opt for the hill country on the edge of the Pennines west of Sheffield and Barnsley. Others will prefer the gentler gradients around Doncaster and Rotherham which, despite the extensive motorway network, contains a maze of peaceful byways. A suitably geared bicycle will cope easily on these different terrains and if the going gets too tough you can always dismount and enjoy a pleasant walk! Cycling around South Yorkshire should be a pleasure, interspersed with halts for rest and refreshments. Details of places of interest as well as cafes, public houses and shops are given in the route itineraries.

The routes have all been researched and ridden by the author himself with not only professionals but beginners and families in mind. They can be shortened or lengthened as required, the more experienced even linking two routes together for a full days ride.

As far as possible the routes keep to traffic-free byroads, sometimes using a short bridleway or off-highway road. Main roads are only used when starting out from, or returning to, a town or where no alternative byroad is available. The routes also include intermediate and total mileages, gradients and things to see along the way.

Have an enjoyable and a safe ride,

Arnold Robinson

Advice Before Setting Out

- The route maps will enable the reader to follow the itinerary but it is recommended that you take the relevant Ordnance Survey 1:50,000 (Landranger) or 1:25,000 (Pathfinder) map. Waterproofed versions are available from your local stockist or in case of difficulty from NMD (Tel: 0114 - 2582660).

- The routes all start in either a suburb of Sheffield or close to the centre of Barnsley, Rotherham and Doncaster, each of which has a British Rail station. Check in advance any arrangements for transporting your bicycle by train. Senior citizens resident in South Yorkshire and families using railcards can travel very economically.

- Parking facilities are given close to the starting point of each ride. The maximum amount of time can then be spent on the actual route itself.

- Ensure your bicycle is in good working order, the saddle and handlebars set correctly for comfort, tyres pumped to the correct pressure, brakes and lights working and all nuts and bolts secure.

- Always carry a pump and puncture repair kit including tyre levers and a spare inner tube. A punctured inner tube can always be repaired on your return home.

- Spare warm clothing and/or waterproofs in case of inclement weather. These are best kept in a pannier rather than a haversack, for safety reasons.

- It is advisable to take a snack and a drink when out for any length of time.

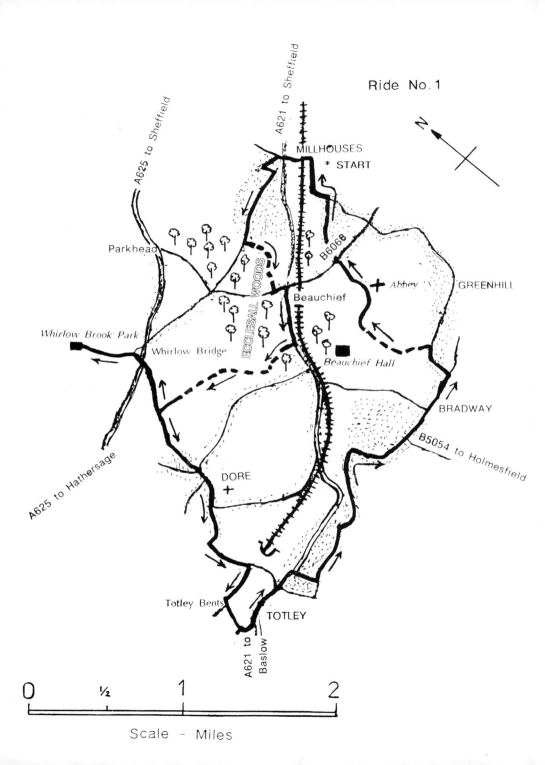

Ride No.1

MILLHOUSES, WHIRLOW, DORE, BRADWAY and BEAUCHIEF

"Bluebells, Crucibles and a Norman Abbey"

Start: Millhouses, on A621, 4 miles SW of Sheffield City Centre.
Car Parking: Millhouses Park
Maps: OS Landranger 110 & 111, OS Pathfinder 743.

This is a short ride ideal for beginners or for riding with children. It starts through some residential suburbs on the south west side of the city and includes some delightful countryside. A bridleway is followed through Ecclesall Woods ending at the attractive Whirlow Brook Park. The return is through some of the older parts of Dore and Totley after which the route climbs to Bradway before turning to Beauchief Abbey. Less than one mile of the ride is along a main road.

GRADIENTS:
Variable. The steepest climbs are from Totley Bents to Baslow Road and from Queen Victoria Road to Bradway.

Miles	Places and Route Itinerary	Information and Points of Interest
0	**MILLHOUSES** At the traffic lights turn into Springfield Road then turn left into Millhouses Lane; in 200 yds turn left (Knaresborough Road) then turn right (Whirlowdale Road); continue ahead and on entering woods turn left (Bridleway) through:	Public House and Shops. Suffered damage by bombing in an air raid in 1940. Pleasant residential area.
	ECCLESALL WOODS Continue through woods to junction of Abbey Lane; turn left and descend to traffic lights at:	A large area of woodlands with a wide variety of trees and wild life. Bluebells grow in profusion in spring. Watch out for the charcoal burner's grave. The woods are divided into three sections each of which is crossed by a network of bridleways and footpaths. The bridleways are unsurfaced but can be ridden without difficulty.
1.5	**BEAUCHIEF** Turn right (Abbeydale Road South) to:	Public House and Shops.

Miles	Places and Route Itinerary	Information and Points of Interest
	ABBEYDALE INDUSTRIAL HAMLET	A unique water-powered scythe-works using 'Crucible' steel and now preserved as a Industrial Museum. Special demonstrations on 'Working Days' advertised locally. Open daily except Christmas Day. Cafe.
	Continue past: **BEAUCHIEF DAM** then continue to:	Provided water power for the work-shops and is now home to a variety of ducks and wild life.
	BEAUCHIEF GARDENS Turn right opposite Gardens into Ecclesall Woods (signposted Bridleway to Dore); in 500 yds turn left across bridge (Rycroft Brook) and then turn right; climb steadily and continue straight ahead to the T-junction (Limb Lane); turn right and continue to the T-junction (Hathersage Road); turn right and immediately turn left to:	A small garden beautifully laid out with flowers and shrubs. The stream is the Porter which feeds the Dam and then continues into the centre of Sheffield where it joins the River Don.
	WHIRLOW BRIDGE Turn left through gate into:	Formerly a sharp bend on the Sheffield-Hathersage Road and once a meeting place for the CTC and other local cycling clubs riding into the Peak District. In spring there is a fine display of daffodils.
2	**WHIRLOW BROOK PARK** Continue through park to House and then retrace route to gate and Hathersage Road; turn right then left (Limb Lane); continue ahead and after short climb descend to the T-junction; turn right then left into:	A beautiful location. The House and Park were acquired by the local authority in 1951. There is a fine display of rhododendrons in June, and a delightful water garden.
1.5	**DORE** Turn left immediately before Hare and Hounds Inn, continue to green; turn right past War Memorial and Church; at the T-junction turn left and continue ahead then descend steeply (Old Hay Lane); at foot of hill immediately before Crown Inn, turn right (Penny Lane); climb past Cricketer's Arms to:	Public House and Shops. Formerly a Derbyshire village taken into Sheffield in the early thirties. Although there has been considerable housing development in recent years, Dore still retains its village atmos-phere. It gained a place in history when in AD829 King Egbert of Wessex met King Eanred of Northumbria here, in consequence of which a united Britain was formed (see plaque on village green). Annual Derbyshire custom of Well Dressings.

Miles	Places and Route Itinerary	Information and Points of Interest
1	**TOTLEY BENTS** Turn left (Lane Head Road) and then climb steeply to a T-junction (Baslow Road); turn left and descend to:	A secluded hamlet on the edge of the moors near to the county boundary with Derbyshire.
0.5	**TOTLEY** Continue ahead and in 500 yds turn right (Main Avenue); then turn left (Green Oak Road); continue to junction (Mickley Lane); turn right and in 200 yds turn left (Queen Victoria Road); fork right (Woodlands Place) and climb very steeply then continue ahead (Prospect Road) to crossroads (B5052); turn left into:	Public House and Shops. Like Dore, Totley was once a Derbyshire village. Parts of the old village still remain away from the A621 main road.
2	**BRADWAY** Continue ahead and in 400 yds turn left (Bradway Road); in further 400 yds at Lodge, turn left into Beauchief Drive; descend past Golf Course and entrance to Beauchief Hall; continue ahead and descend past:	Shops. Bradway was also transferred from Derbyshire into Sheffield in the thirties. There has been extensive housing development although a little of the old village remains. Beauchief Hall was formerly a Roman Catholic School.
1.5	**BEAUCHIEF ABBEY** Continue to crossroads (Abbey Lane); continue ahead (Folds Lane) and after short climb continue ahead and join Hutcliffe Wood Road; descend through Hutcliffe Wood then turn left across railway bridge to:	In a beautiful setting below woods which stretch along a ridge and where a stream running down from the hills feeds two ponds. Little remains of the Norman abbey although the tower is impressive and rises above the greens of the Municipal Golf Course. Inside the small church is a two decker pulpit, some box pews and a monument. Services are still held here.
1	**MILLHOUSES**	End.

The ruined Norman Abbey at Beauchief (Ride 1)

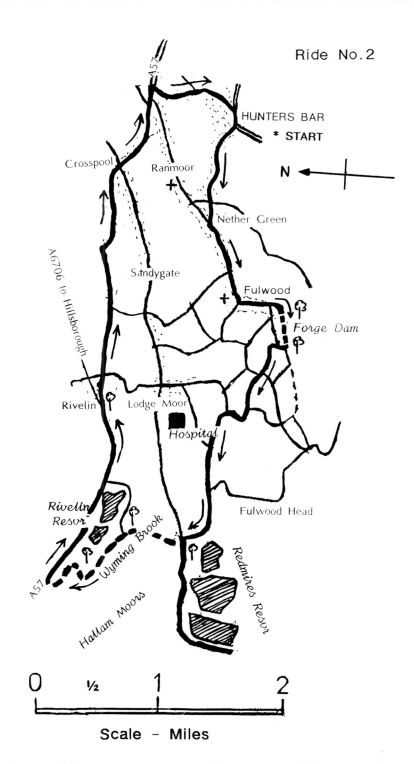

Ride No.2

HUNTERS BAR
* START

N

Crosspool
Ranmoor
A57

Nether Green

A6706 to Hillsborough

Sandygate

Fulwood

Forge Dam

Rivelin
Lodge Moor

Hospital

Fulwood Head

Rivelin
Resvr

Wyming Brook

A57

Hallam Moors

Redmires Resvr

0   ½   1   2

Scale - Miles

HUNTERS BAR, FULWOOD, REDMIRES, RIVELIN and CROSSPOOL

"Water Wheels, Reservoirs and a Glimpse of the Moors"

Start: Hunters Bar, Ecclesall Road or alternatively Broomhill.
Car Parking: Rustlings Road alongside Endcliffe Park.
Maps: OS Landranger 110, OS Pathfinder 743.

This short route explores the lovely countryside to the west of Sheffield with its marvellous scenery and extensive views of moorland and wooded ravines. It is suitable for a half-day or evening ride and provides an opportunity to see the Redmires and Rivelin Reservoirs.

GRADIENTS:
There are a few hilly sections, the most strenuous being the climb from Nether Green to Fulwood Church, out of the Mayfield Valley and from Rivelin Post office to Crosspool.

Miles	Places and Route Itinerary	Information and Points of Interest
0	**HUNTERS BAR** Leave by Ecclesall Road and in 500 yds turn right (Rustlings Road); fork left (Oakbrook Road) and at traffic lights continue straight ahead (Nether Green Road) and climb to:	Suburban shopping centre and traffic usually busy. Endcliffe Park on right with cafe and memorial to the crew of a crashed World War II bomber.
1.5	**NETHER GREEN** Fork left (Fulwood Road) and climb steeply in parts to:	Shops and residential area. Almost continuous climb to Fulwood Church.
0.5	**FULWOOD CHURCH** Fork left (Brooklands Hill) and descend; at crossroads turn left and in 200 yds continue straight ahead on a narrow byroad *"No Through Road"*. Descend and cross the stream and fork right to:	The former village has been extended by modern housing but is still a very pleasant part of the city. Shops.
0.5	**FORGE DAM** Retrace route and turn left (Whiteley Lane) climb and turn left (Quiet Lane); descend and fork right (Mayfield Road); climb through:	Cafe, toilets and a Childrens Playground. The dam originally supplied water power for a forge. Ancient chapel on right, built 1728.

Miles	Places and Route Itinerary	Information and Points of Interest
1	**MAYFIELD VALLEY** Continue ahead and in half mile at the T-junction turn right (Gorse Lane); climb steeply and turn left (Brown Hills Lane); continue ahead through open countryside (Roughley Lane); after right turn, descend to the T-junction (Redmires Road); turn left and descend to head of:	A narrow lane climbs through a quiet and pleasant valley passing former Mayfield School on right. Lodge Moor Hospital on right and views of Hallam Moors ahead.
1.5	**WYMING BROOK DRIVE** Continue ahead and climb alongside:	Picturesque spot ideal for picnics.
0.5	**REDMIRES RESERVOIRS** to end of surfaced road; retrace route and turn left alongside:	Three small reservoirs. On left is a stone sign removed from the former 'Grouse & Trout' Inn which was demolished in 1950.
1	**WYMING BROOK DRIVE** Descend through woods and continue to the T-junction (A57 Manchester Road); at:	A Water Board drive which is unsurfaced but rideable with care. It is a delightful cycling route through woods with occasional glimpses of streams and the two Rivelin Dams.
2	**HOLLOW MEADOWS** Turn right and descend to:	Cafe. Busy road care required.
2	**RIVELIN BRIDGE** Fork right (Manchester Road) and climb to:	Cafe. Camping and Caravan Site. Long climb with a view of the Rivelin valley.
2	**CROSSPOOL** Continue ahead and descend to:	Shops. The highest residential suburb of Sheffield.
1	**BROOMHILL** Fork left (Fulwood Road) then turn right (Glossop Road); in 200 yds turn right (Westbourne Road); descend to the T-junction; turn right (Brocco Bank) and descend to:	
1	**HUNTERS BAR**	End.

A stone sign from the now demolished "Grouse and Trout" Inn
along the road to the Redmires Reservoirs (Ride 2)

The Redmires Reservoirs (Ride 2)

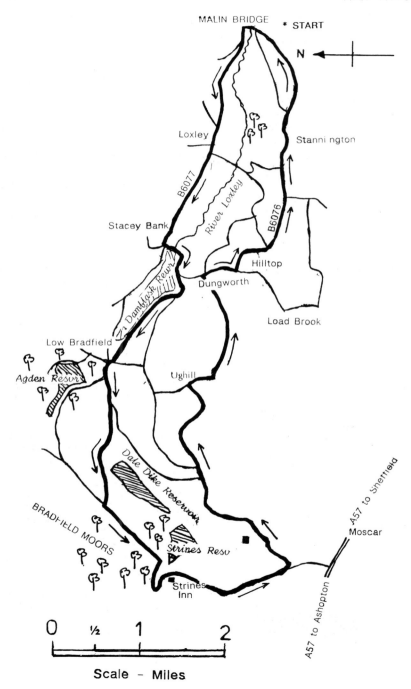

MALIN BRIDGE   * START

N

Loxley

Stannington

B6077

River Loxley

Stacey Bank

B6076

Damflask Resvr.

Hilltop

Dungworth

Load Brook

Low Bradfield

Ughill

Agden Resvr.

Dale Dike Reservoir

BRADFIELD MOORS

Strines Resv.

Moscar

A57 to Sheffield

A57 to Ashopton

Strines
Inn

0   ½   1   2

Scale - Miles

MALIN BRIDGE, LOXLEY, BRADFIELD, STRINES and DUNGWORTH

"Rivers, Reservoirs and Robin Hood"

Start: Malin Bridge (Terminus of Sheffield Super-Tram).
Maps: OS Landranger 110, OS Pathfinder 726 & 743.

The ride starts by following the valley of the River Loxley which flows from the reservoirs above Bradfield and joins the River Don at Owlerton. The route then climbs to the hills which encircle the head of the Valley and from which there are some marvellous views including the Emley Moor Television Transmitter high on the Pennines. From Strines Moor, the return is made along quiet byroads through Ughill and Dungworth before descending to Stannington.

GRADIENTS:
The first few miles are relatively easy but after Low Bradfield the route climbs to the edge of the moors. There is a steep climb to the Strines Inn after which the gradients vary ending with an easy descent back to Malin Bridge.

Miles	Places and Route Itinerary	Information and Points of Interest
0	**MALIN BRIDGE** Turn right (Loxley Road) and immediately bear left; climb gently to:	Shops. Here the River Rivelin and River Loxley converge at the foot of the picturesque Rivelin Valley. There is an old mill here.
1	**LOXLEY** Continue ahead through:	Claimed to be the birthplace of Robin Hood and formerly a West Riding village but now an outer suburb of Sheffield.
1.5	**STACEY BANK** In a half mile turn left then bear right along the south side of Damflask reservoir; after a short climb continue to a T-junction; turn right and descend to:	Small hamlet on the approach to Damflask Reservoir on the eastern boundary of the Peak District National Park. Water sports take place on the reservoir and there are fine views of the Pennine Hills.
2.5	**LOW BRADFIELD** Fork left and after a short climb continue on a narrow byroad which climbs through the valley to:	Pleasant village with a public house and a picturesque cricket ground. Several byroads climb steeply up to the moors.

Miles	Places and Route Itinerary	Information and Points of Interest
2	**Junction of STRINES ROAD** Turn left and descend to bridge then climb very steeply to:	Exciting byroad from A57 near Moscar which continues northwards to Langsett.
1.5	**STRINES INN** Continue ahead across open moor and immediately after cattle grid, turn left; continue ahead past Sugworth Hall; bear right at two junctions and descend to:	An ancient and welcoming former coaching inn on the moors near to the county boundary. A tower known as Boot's Folly was built by the local unemployed.
4.5	**UGHILL** Descend steeply and turn right then climb and continue to a T-junction; turn right and climb through:	A remote hamlet in a fold of hills above Damflask Reservoir.
2	**DUNGWORTH** Continue ahead and after a further climb, descend through:	A small village in an exposed position on the hillside above the Loxley valley.
2	**STANNINGTON** Continue through the village and descend to:	A large suburb with some modern housing.
2	**MALIN BRIDGE**	End.

The Chapel of St. James at Midhopestones (Ride 4)

Boot's Folly Tower above Strines Reservoir   (Ride 3)

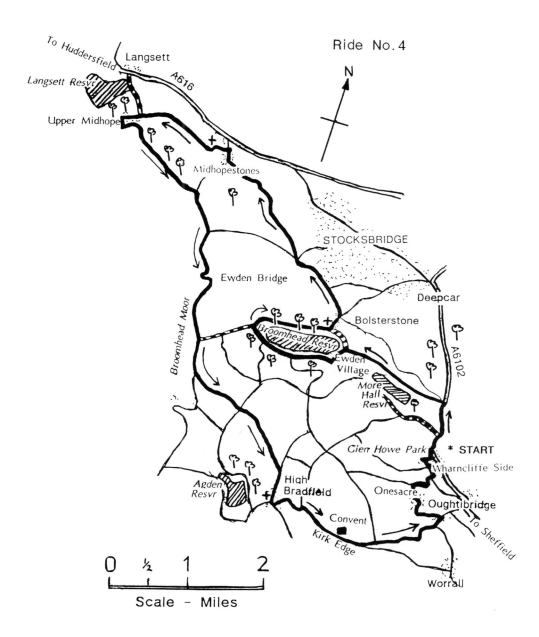

Ride No. 4

N

To Huddersfield Langsett
A616
Langsett Resvr
Upper Midhope
Midhopestones
STOCKSBRIDGE
Ewden Bridge
Deepcar
Broomhead Moor
Broomhead Resvr
Bolsterstone
A6102
Ewden Village
More Hall Resvr
Glen Howe Park
START
Wharncliffe Side
Agden Resvr
High Bradfield
Onesacre
Oughtibridge
Convent
To Sheffield
Kirk Edge
Worrall

0   ½   1   2

Scale - Miles

Ride No. 4   21.5 Miles

WHARNCLIFFE SIDE, EWDEN, MIDHOPE, BRADFIELD and OUGHTIBRIDGE

"Wooded Ravines, Ancient Villages and a Bodysnatcher's Watch House"

Start: Glen Howe Park, Wharncliffe Side, on A6102 seven miles NW of Sheffield.
Car Parking: Glen Howe Park.
Maps: OS Landranger 110, OS Pathfinder 726.

This is one of the finest scenic routes in South Yorkshire. After the first mile along the A6102 the whole of the ride is along quiet byroads but it should be stressed that many of them are hilly as they climb along the eastern edge of the Pennines, often in and out of ravines. There are some alternative routes which avoid some of the steeper gradients. Throughout the ride there are extensive and ever changing views. From the junction at Upper Midhope, there is an optional diversion to Langsett where there are Tea Rooms which are very popular with cyclists.

GRADIENTS:
The most severe climbs are (a) from Broomhead Reservoir to Bolsterstone; (b) up to Upper Midhope; (c) from Ewden to Broomhead Moor; and (d) on the byroad through Onesacre when returning to Glen Howe Park.

Miles	Places and Route Itinerary	Information and Points of Interest
0	**GLEN HOWE PARK** Take the track at the side of the Car Park and turn left on joining the surfaced byroad; descend to the T-junction (A6102) at:	A beautiful park in a wooded ravine. Cycling is not permitted but a walk is recommended. Rebuilt packhorse bridge over the brook. The park was a gift of Joseph Dixon, a local industrialist. Ideal for picnics.
0.5	**WHARNCLIFFE SIDE** Turn left and after climbing for a half mile (see note (a) below), descend to bridge then turn left through a gate on the Water Board drive; continue through woods to:	A small straggling village on the Sheffield-Stocksbridge road. The Water Board Drive is a delightful cycling route through woods and alongside More Hall Reservoir.
2.5	**EWDEN** At cross roads turn left; cross bridge and in 50 yds turn right through a gate on the bridleway; after a short climb continue alongside the reservoir; on leaving the bridleway turn right on a byroad and at the T-junction in half-mile turn right (see note (b) below) continue through woods and climb steeply to:	A Water Board village in a beautiful location. The Youth Hostel was closed in 1966. The Bridleway, most of which can be ridden, provides a view of the upper part of the Ewden Valley and hills beyond. A road to the left climbs to Wigtwizzle and Broomhead Moor.

Miles	Places and Route Itinerary	Information and Points of Interest
3	**BOLSTERSTONE** Fork left (signposted Midhopestones) and continue through outskirts of Deepcar; in one-mile fork right and descend; after a short climb continue to a T-junction and turn right to:	Shops. A hilltop village which is the 'home' of the Bolsterstone Male Voice Choir. Stone cottages are grouped around the church outside which are some stocks.
3	**MIDHOPESTONES** Turn left at the Inn and climb past the church; continue on a narrow byroad then climb to the junction at the outskirts of:	A small community, mainly farms, set aside from the busy A616. The 17th century St. James' Church has a Jacobean pulpit, box pews and a gallery.
1.5	**UPPER MIDHOPE** (See note (c) below). Continue ahead through the village; turn left and after a winding descent, continue to a T-junction; turn right and in one mile start a *very steep descent* to:	A remote hilltop village of farms and stone cottages. 'Cut Gate' is a moorland crossing to the Derwent Valley.
3.5	**EWDEN BRIDGE** Climb *very steeply* through woods and then continue an easier climb; in one mile fork left at an ancient milestone; at the cross-roads continue ahead and after a short climb descend to:	A lovely wooded ravine, the descent of which is very steep with sharp turns at the foot. Care is required. This is followed by a strenuous climb out of the valley. The shorter route (see note (b) below) joins the main route here.
4	**BRADFIELD** Fork left and immediately turn left; climb steeply then continue along the ridge road past:	This is High Bradfield to distinguish it from Low Bradfield in the valley below. It is a small village of stone cottages. The church occupies a prominent position on the hilltop and has a turret-like building which once housed watchmen who guarded fresh graves from bodysnatchers.
1	**KIRK EDGE CONVENT** In a half mile, fork left; descend steeply to outskirts of:	Road runs along the ridge giving extensive views. For direct route to Sheffield, continue straight ahead through Worrall.
1.5	**OUGHTIBRIDGE** Shortly after passing turn on right to Worrall, turn very sharp left into a narrow byroad (Wheel Lane) alongside Coombs Brook; climb *very steeply* (1 in 4) to:	Main part of village is at the foot of the hill on the Sheffield-Stocksbridge road. Shops. *Do not overshoot* the turn on to Wheel Lane which is not obvious.

Miles	Places and Route Itinerary	Information and Points of Interest
1	**ONESACRE** At the T-junction turn left (Green Lane) and continue climbing; in a half mile fork right (signposted Wharncliffe Side); descend *very steeply* (acute bend) and at T-junction turn left; continue descent and fork left in:	A delightful hamlet of stone cottages on a hillside. This ancient village once had a school which was closed in 1886. Views across Don Valley to Wharncliffe Woods.
1	**GLEN HOWE PARK**	End.

NOTES:

(a)   There is a slightly shorter but hillier alternative way by turning left on the climb from Wharncliffe Side. This climbs to the hamlet of Brightholmlee but omits the ride along the Water Board Drive.

(b)   By turning left and climbing along the Broomhead Reservoir to Wigtwizzle, the main route is joined at Broomhead Moor. This is a much shorter route (total mileage 14) but it omits some beautiful countryside.

(c)   At the junction on the outskirts of Upper Midhope, a right turn leads to Langsett. Shops, public house and Bank View Cafe, popular with cyclists from both sides of the Pennines. (One and a half miles return).

The Bodysnatcher's Watch House at High Bradfield   (Ride 4)

23

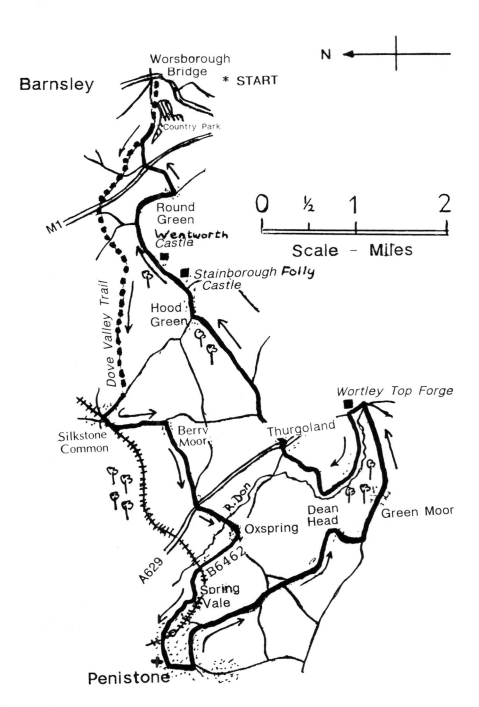

WORSBROUGH, SILKSTONE, PENISTONE, WORTLEY and HOOD GREEN

"A Flour Mill, a Disused Railway and a Folly Castle"

Start: Worsbrough Mill.
Car Parking: Worsbrough Mill Pay & Display Car Park or Kendal Green Crossing on Haverland Lane.
Maps: OS Landranger 110, OS Pathfinder 715 & 726.

The first four miles are along the Dove Valley Trail, a former railway track now converted to a cycling and walking route. The route then crosses into the valley of the Upper Don and from Oxspring continues to Penistone. The ride then climbs over the hills to Greenmoor, the highest point of the ride, before returning to the Don Valley.

GRADIENTS:

The ride along the Dove Valley Trail is easy but there are then several climbs, none of them too long. The return from Thurgoland is mainly a long descent.

Miles	Places and Route Itinerary	Information and Points of Interest
0	**WORSBROUGH BRIDGE** At Car Park exit, turn left (Park Road) and immediately turn left through a gate to join the:	Worsbrough Flour Mill, built in c.1625, is now a working museum open to the public.
	DOVE VALLEY TRAIL In a half mile cross a byroad (Kendal Green Crossing) and continue on the Trail; in one mile cross a bridge (M1) and continue into open country; in two and a half miles turn right and descend a slope to a gate; turn right on to byroad and climb to:	The Trail makes for excellent off-highway cycling with a smooth surface and an easy gradient. There are several scenic stretches. There are interesting stone sculptures close to the exit to Silkstone Common.
4	**SILKSTONE COMMON** At cross-roads (B6449) turn left and continue to:	A small hilltop village with shops, a public house and a railway station.
1	**BERRY MOOR** Fork right and climb, steeply at times, then descend to a cross-roads (A629); continue straight ahead and descend; cross bridge (River Don) and immediately turn right (Roughbirch-worth Road); climb to:	A hamlet at the junction where the road to Thurgoland turns off to the left. The A629 is a busy main road so care is required when crossing.

Miles	Places and Route Itinerary	Information and Points of Interest
1.5	**OXSPRING** At the cross-roads (B6462) turn right and continue through:	A small village in the Don Valley. Shops.
1.5	**SPRING VALE** Continue ahead and climb into:	A suburb of Penistone, part residential with some light industry.
1	**PENISTONE** At the junction in the centre of town, turn left and in a half mile turn left (Green Lane); descend and turn right (Castle Road); after a short climb continue through open country; in one mile turn right; at cross-roads continue straight ahead along high ground and descend through:	Most of the industry has left the town which is now a quiet, mainly rural centre. Shops, railway station, market on Thursday, early closing Tuesday, cafe.
3	**DEAN HEAD** Climb to a T-junction and turn left; descend through:	Extensive views.
1	**GREEN MOOR** Continue to descend steeply at times, to a T-junction; turn left (signposted Thurgoland) past:	A small village on a ridge above the Don Valley. Wide views, stocks and a public house.
1.5	**WORTLEY TOP FORGE** Continue ahead, cross a bridge (River Don) and immediately turn left (Old Mill Lane); in one mile climb steeply then after a short descent, again climb to a T-junction (B6462); turn right and immediately turn left to cross-roads (junction A629); continue straight ahead (Roper Road); after a short climb descend through outskirts of:	A preserved 17th century industrial site with limited opening hours.
1.5	**THURGOLAND** Turn left and start a long descent; ignoring all side turns to:	A small hilltop village on the Sheffield to Huddersfield road. Shops.
2	**HOOD GREEN** Bear to the right through the village and then fork left (Lowe Lane); descend steeply at times to:	Stainborough Castle is a folly in the woods on the right, built by a previous owner of Wentworth Castle, now a College.
1.5	**STAINBOROUGH** Continue straight ahead (Round Green Lane) and after a short climb turn left through:	Note the unusual Steeple Lodge at the entrance is disguised to look like a country church.

Miles	Places and Route Itinerary	Information and Points of Interest
1	**ROUND GREEN** Pass under a bridge (M1) and continue to Kendal Green Crossing; continue ahead to a T-junction (Vernon Road); turn right and in 50 yds at a T-junction turn right (Park Road) to:	A farm with a herd of deer.
1	**WORSBROUGH MILL**	End.

The Steeple Lodge at the entrance to Wentworth Castle (Ride 5)

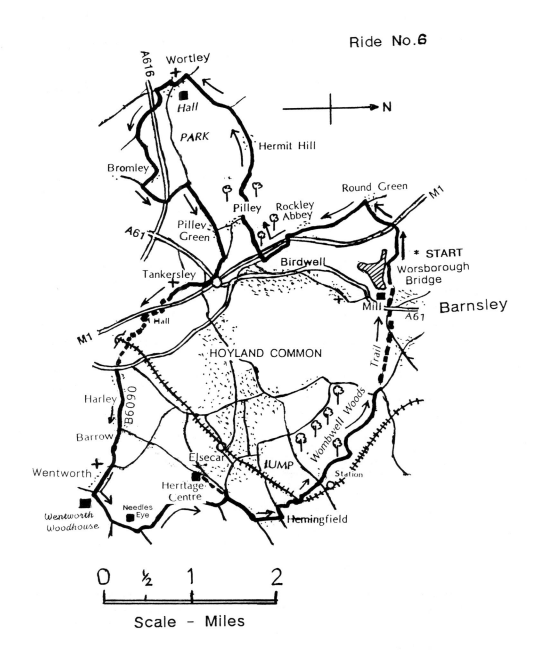

Ride No.6

Ride No. 6   24 Miles

WORSBROUGH, WORTLEY, TANKERSLEY, WENTWORTH and ELSECAR

"Steep Climbs, Steam Engines and some Delightful Villages"

Start: Worsbrough Bridge, off A61, one and a half miles south of Barnsley.
Car Parking: Worsbrough Mill Pay & Display Car Park.
Maps: OS Landranger 111, OS Pathfinder 715 & 726.

To the south of Barnsley, it is possible – by careful map reading – to select some excellent cycling routes which avoid built up areas and the many main roads. As the map shows, the route weaves about but it can be very enjoyable, especially at weekends.

GRADIENTS:
The first part of the route is very hilly. Between Roundgreen and Wortley there are some steep climbs and descents on which care is required. The return to Wentworth and Elsecar is much easier but there are then more climbs through Hemingfield.

Miles	Places and Route Itinerary	Information and Points of Interest
0	**WORSBROUGH BRIDGE** At the Car Park Exit, turn left (Park Road) and in 150 yds turn left through a gate and on to:	Worsbrough Flour Mill, built in c.1625, is now a working museum open to the public.
	DOVE VALLEY TRAIL Continue to first exit at Kendall Crossing then leave Trail and turn left on byroad; continue ahead and pass under bridge (M1); climb through:	The Trail makes for excellent off-highway cycling with a smooth surface and an easy gradient.
1.5	**ROUNDGREEN** At the T-junction turn left (see note (a) below); continue ahead and then descend passing:	A farming hamlet and deer farm. Very quiet despite being so close to the M1 motorway. In the field on the right is the Queen Anne Obelisk erected by an owner of Wentworth Castle.
1.0	**ROCKLEY ABBEY** Pass under the bridge (M1) and climb steeply; in a half mile turn right (signposted Pilley); after a short descent climb steeply to:	The byroad climbs alongside the motorway past Birdwell and another obelisk giving directions to Wentworth Castle.

Miles	Places and Route Itinerary	Information and Points of Interest
1.5	**PILLEY** At the T-junction turn right and in a half mile descend steeply (very sharp bend) then climb through:	A former colliery village but little evidence now remains of the mine.
1.0	**HERMIT HILL** Continue climbing and fork left then continue climbing to a T-junction (A629); turn left into:	A hamlet with many picturesque cottages straggling along the byroad.
1.5	**WORTLEY** Turn right past the church (see note (b) below); at the cross-roads continue ahead and cross the bridge (A616 Stocksbridge By-Pass); immediately turn left (signposted Howbrook) and descend on the byroad; in a half-mile turn left on a narrow byroad and continue to descend to:	Cafe (Closed Monday and Tuesday). Pleasantly situated on A629 where this turns sharply past St. Leonard's Church. Note the lychgate and coffin table. Highest point of the ride. Also see Ride No. 8.
2.0	**BROMLEY** At Green, fork left and continue to descend; at the T-junction turn left and after a further short descent, climb under the bridge (A616) then continue through woods; then descend through:	A small picturesque village with a green.
2.5	**PILLEY GREEN** Continue to descend (New Road) and pass under the bridge (A61); climb to the T-junction and turn right (Tankersley Road); then fork left past:	An extension of the village of Pilley.
1.5	**TANKERSLEY CHURCH** Continue on unsurfaced byroad; pass under the subway (M1) and continue to:	The church stands in a remote situation and contains cannon balls from the Civil War Battle of Tankersley Moor.
1.0	**TANKERSLEY OLD HALL** Turn left at the farm entrance and continue on an unsurfaced road to cross-roads (A61) and continue ahead (signposted B6090 Wentworth) to:	The 16th century Hall, now in ruins having been abandoned when the last owner died leaving no heir, was used as a filming location for the film "Kes" in which the lead was played by a local boy. Take care when crossing the main road.
1.0	**HARLEY** Continue ahead then climb through:	A small wayside village with shops and a public house. Ruins of a windmill on the left.
1.0	**BARROW** Continue into:	A former Toll House on right and almshouses on the left.

Miles	Places and Route Itinerary	Information and Points of Interest
0.5	**WENTWORTH** Continue through the village and in a half-mile turn left on byroad (Coley Lane); climb and after a short descent; turn left (signposted Elsecar); descend and at foot of hill turn left to the T-junction (B6097); turn left across bridge and immediately turn left through gate on to Trail, and continue to:	One of many delightful South Yorkshire villages, containing two churches, one of which is in ruins. The newer church has a prominent spire visible over a wide area. Wentworth Woodhouse, formerly the seat of the Fitzwilliam family, is an impressive building with the longest country house frontage in Europe. Cycling is not permitted in the park. On left of Coley Lane is the Needles' Eye folly erected as a bet by the Marquess of Rockingham.
2.5	**ELSECAR Heritage Centre** Retrace route along Trail to a T-junction (B6097); turn right and in a half-mile turn left; climb into:	Industrial workshops, Steam Railway Centre, National Bottle Museum and a Newcomen Beam Engine. Cafe.
1.5	**HEMINGFIELD** Climb to a T-junction and turn left then fork right; climb steeply then continue to cross-roads at:	A small village on the hillside.
1.0	**WOMBWELL STATION** Continue straight ahead (Dovecliff Road) and continue through:	A railway station. The centre of Wombwell is one mile north-east.
	WOMBWELL WOODS Climb then descend and turn right (Station Road); descend steeply (sharp bend) and at the foot of the hill, turn left through a gate and on to:	Although so close to industry the ride through the woods is very pleasant especially in the summer and autumn.
	DOVE VALLEY TRAIL Continue along Trail to second exit; turn left on B6100 West Street and continue to a T-junction (A61) turn left to:	See above.
3.0	**WORSBROUGH MILL**	End.

NOTES:

(a) Alternative route: turn right and climb past Wentworth Castle to Hood Green; here turn left and after descent and another climb, join above route on approach to Wortley. Distance approximately the same.

(b) From the centre of Wortley, there is an alternative route to Pilley Green through Wortley Park.

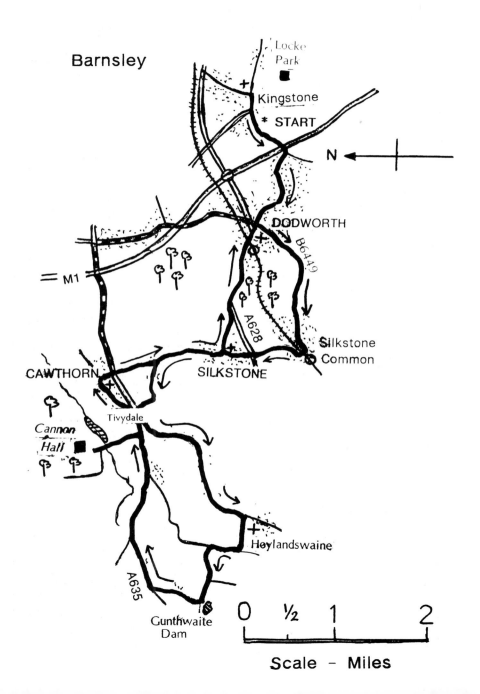

Barnsley

Locke Park

Kingstone

* START

N

DODWORTH

B6449

M1

A628

Silkstone
Common

CAWTHORN

SILKSTONE

Tivydale

Cannon
Hall

Heylandswaine

A635

Gunthwaite
Dam

0   ½   1   2

Scale - Miles

Ride No. 7   19 Miles

BARNSLEY, DODWORTH, SILKSTONE, GUNTHWAITE and CAWTHORNE

"Quiet Country Lanes, Peaceful Villages and a Country House"

Start: Kingstone on A6133, one mile west of Barnsley.
Alternative start from Worsbrough Mill (See note (a) below)
Car Parking: Locke Park, Kersforth Hall Road.
Maps: OS Landranger 110, OS Pathfinder 715.

This ride around the byways to the west of Barnsley is without question one of the best in the area both for interest and for scenic attractions. The lanes in the vicinity of Gunthwaite Dam are delightful. Cannon Hall and the adjoining country park, and the nearby village of Cawthorne are highlights. If they were in a more popular touring area such as the Cotswolds, they would undoubtedly be crowded with visitors. For the moment, they can be enjoyed in relative peace.

GRADIENTS:
After a steady climb from Dodworth to Silkstone Common there is a descent to Silkstone. From Tivy Dale junction there is then a long climb to Hoylandswaine. Most of the remainder of the ride is gently undulating.

Miles	Places and Route Itinerary	Information and Points of Interest
0	**KINGSTONE** Take A6133 west and in a half-mile fork left (B6099); descend steeply, cross the bridge (M1) and climb into:	A residential suburb of Barnsley with an interesting church. Close by is Locke Park, with its ornate tower, bequeathed to Barnsley in memory of local railway engineer Joseph Locke.
2	**DODWORTH** At the cross-roads turn left at the War Memorial (Green Road) and climb steadily to:	A former mining community, the mine is now closed. The colliery once had a very successful brass band. Railway station.
2	**SILKSTONE COMMON** At the cross-roads turn right under the railway bridge and then turn right; descend to the staggered cross-roads; turn right and then left into:	A small hilltop community with a railway station on the Barnsley – Huddersfield line.
1	**SILKSTONE** Continue through the village and at the junction by the church fork left on a byroad; in one mile after a short climb turn left (Norcroft Lane) and in a half mile turn right and descend to the junction at:	A pleasant village now bypassed by the A628 Barnsley–Manchester road. Public House and old stocks. The ancient church is part Norman with buttresses and gargoyles, an oak roof, box pews, screens and monuments. A monument in the churchyard is to 26 children drowned when the Huskar pit was flooded in 1838. They included 7 boys under 10 and a girl aged 8.

Miles	Places and Route Itinerary	Information and Points of Interest
1.5	**TIVY DALE** Turn sharp left (South Lane) and climb for one and a half miles to the outskirts of:	Part of the village of Cawthorne (See below).
2	**HOYLANDSWAINE** Turn right (Cross Lane) and in a half-mile at the T-junction turn right; descend and take the next turn left; descend then climb to the junction at:	A hilltop village.
1.5	**GUNTHWAITE DAM** Turn sharp right and climb for a half-mile; at the T-junction turn right then descend to the T-junction (A653); turn right and after climbing past the brick works descend and take the next turn left (signposted Cannon Hall); descend to the bridge and turn right through the Car Park to:	Quiet lanes lead to a small lake in a pleasant woodland setting. A peaceful spot with some wildlife. Close by is the superb 16th century Gunthwaite tithe barn.
3	**CANNON HALL** Retrace the route across the bridge and climb to the T-junction (A653); turn left and descend to cross-roads; turn left through:	A beautiful setting in parkland which slopes down to lakes where there is an attractive bridge with stone ballustrading. The Hall, formerly the seat of the Spencer-Stanhopes, is now a country museum which includes the Regimental Museum of the 13/15th Hussars. There is a cafe in the grounds and at the nearby Garden Centre.
1	**TIVY DALE** Continue ahead and climb into:	
0.5	**CAWTHORNE** Turn right in the centre of the village and at the crossroads (A653) continue straight ahead on the byroad (signposted Silkstone); continue ahead and climb to the outskirts of:	Public House and shops. A beautifully situated and attractive village bypassed by the A635 Barnsley-Holmfirth road. Picturesque stone cottages and an old cross with Saxon carving. The church contains the mausoleum of the Spencer-Stanhopes. The village museum is in a Tudor style building once a chapel and contains many local finds including a bomb from the 1939-45 war.

Miles	Places and Route Itinerary	Information and Points of Interest
1.5	**SILKSTONE** Turn left at the church and after a short descent, climb; at the T-junction (A628), continue on; in one mile at the traffic island turn right (signposted Barnsley), after the level crossing when the main road turns left; continue straight ahead into:	See above.
1.5	**DODWORTH** At the cross-roads in the centre of the village continue straight ahead and descend and retrace the outward route; cross the bridge (M1) and climb steeply; at the T-junction (A6133); turn right to:	See above.
1.5	**KINGSTONE**	End.

NOTE:
(a) If starting from Worsbrough Mill, take the Dove Valley Trail to Silkstone Common (see Ride No. 5). To return to Worsbrough Mill, from Kingstone, take Kersforth Hall Road through Ward Green.

The ornate tower in Locke Park, Barnsley (Ride 7)

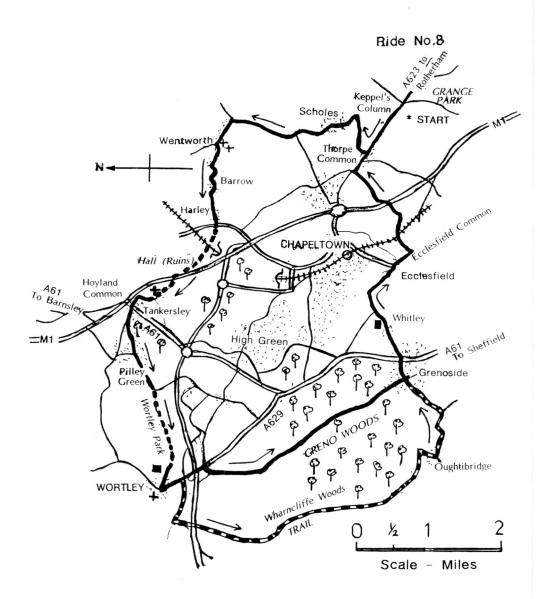

Ride No.8

GRANGE PARK, WENTWORTH, TANKERSLEY, WORTLEY and GRENOSIDE

"Ruins, Sword Dancers and an Elizabethan Hall"

Start: Grange Park, Wortley Road. Off A629, two miles NW of Rotherham.
Car Parking: Grange Park.
MAPS: OS Landranger 110, OS Pathfinder 726.

This ride makes a circuit of rural countryside to the north west of Rotherham including the estate village of Wentworth, the ruins of Tankersley Hall and an off-highway route through Wortley Park. There is an alternative return route through Wharncliffe Woods but this involves a very steep climb to join the main route at Grenoside.
Although never far from built up areas and industry, the route keeps to quiet byroads.

GRADIENTS:
For the most part, the ride is gently undulating. There are a few climbs as indicated in the Route Itinerary, eg. on the approach to Wentworth and from Ecclesfield to Thorpe Common.

Miles	Places and Route Itinerary	Information and Points of Interest
0	**GRANGE PARK** At the exit from the Car Park, turn left on the A629 towards Thorpe Hesley; in a half-mile at the Sportsman Inn, turn right (signposted Scholes) on a narrow byroad; descend (sharp bend) through:	Keppel's Column, 115 ft. high on the right, was erected by the Marquess of Rockingham after his friend Admiral Keppel had been wrongly blamed for a naval defeat against the French. Care when turning right at Sportsman Inn.
2	**SCHOLES** Continue through the village and after a short climb, descend to the T-junction; turn right (signposted Wentworth); climb steeply for one-mile (Haugh Lane) and at T-junction, turn left (B6090) into:	A sprawling village on the byroad to Wentworth. A former ford at the bottom of the hill is now bridged. The Garden Centre on the right has a cafe.
2	**WENTWORTH** Continue along Main Street and then fork left; continue through:	One of many delightful villages in South Yorkshire contains two churches, one of which is in ruins. The newer church has a prominent spire visible over a very wide area. Wentworth Woodhouse, formerly the seat of the Fitzwilliam family, is an impressive building with the longest country house frontage in Europe. Cycling is not permitted in the park.

Miles	Places and Route Itinerary	Information and Points of Interest
0.5	**BARROW** Continue ahead through:	A former Toll House is on the left and almshouses on the right.
0.5	**HARLEY** At the cross-roads (A6135) continue straight ahead on an unsurfaced road; pass under the railway bridge and continue past:	A small wayside village with public house and shops. Take care when crossing the main road.
1	**TANKERSLEY OLD HALL** Continue on the lane and pass through the subway under the M1; climb on a narrow lane past:	The 16th century Hall, now in ruins, having been abandoned when the last owner died leaving no heir, was used as a filming location for the film Kes in which the lead was played by a local boy.
0.5	**TANKERSLEY CHURCH** At the T-junction turn right and after a right-hand bend, turn left (signposted Pilley) alongside the M1; in a half-mile fork left (signposted Pilley Green); climb through:	The church stands in an isolated location and contains cannon balls from the Civil War Battle of Tankersley Moor.
1	**PILLEY GREEN** Climb for one mile and when the road bends left, fork right into:	Once a colliery village, the mine site is now a modern industrial estate.
1	**WORTLEY PARK** Continue on the bridleway (gated) and on leaving the park, continue ahead into:	A pleasant one mile drive through parkland. The surface is rough but most of it is rideable. Some of the gates may be locked but the pedestrian gates can be used. Wortley Hall, on the right, was formerly the seat of the Earls of Wharncliffe and is now a Labour Party Educational Centre and Holiday Home.
1.5	**WORTLEY** Turn left past the church and in a half-mile at the cross-roads, continue ahead; (see note (a) below); in a half-mile cross the bridge (A616 Stocksbridge Bypass); immediately turn right then turn left on a byroad; climb steeply at times and continue along the ridge road; descend through Greno Woods to cross-roads at:	A pleasantly situated village on the A629 where this turns sharply past St. Leonard's church. The highest point of the ride. Take care when turning off A629. There are extensive views to the east.

Miles	Places and Route Itinerary	Information and Points of Interest
3.5	**GRENOSIDE** Turn left opposite the Old Harrow public house (Norfolk Hill); descend to junction with the A629; turn right and immediately turn left (Whitley Lane); descend through:	A former West Riding village now a suburb of Sheffield. Shops. Take care when turning right, view restricted. The Grenoside Sword Dancers perform in the Old Red Lion on Boxing Day, a Yorkshire version of the Morris Dance.
1	**WHITLEY** Continue ahead on a narrow byroad to the T-junction at the outskirts of:	A small farming community with an Elizabethan Hall, picturesquely situated in a wooded valley, which is now a restaurant.
1	**ECCLESFIELD** Turn left to the T-junction (A6235); turn right (The Common); at the traffic lights continue ahead and in a half-mile turn left (Station Road); pass under two railway bridges then climb; turn left (Jumble Lane); cross the bridge (M1) and after a short descent climb to the T-junction at:	The centre of the village is to the right. Shops.
1.5	**THORPE COMMON** Turn right (A629 Upper Wortley Road) and return to:	Shops.
2	**GRANGE PARK**	End.

NOTES:

(a) There is an alternative route from Wortley to Grenoside through Wharncliffe Woods. At the cross-roads on leaving Wortley, turn right; descend for one mile and on the approach to a bridge, turn left (opposite telephone kiosk) into former station yard (station buildings now a private residence); continue on forestry drive through woods; in a half-mile fork right and pass under the sub-way of the A616; continue along the Trail (all rideable) to the junction with the byroad from Oughtibridge to Grenoside; turn left and climb very steeply then descend (St. Stephen's Hill) to the cross-roads at Grenoside; where you rejoin the main route.

Ride No.9

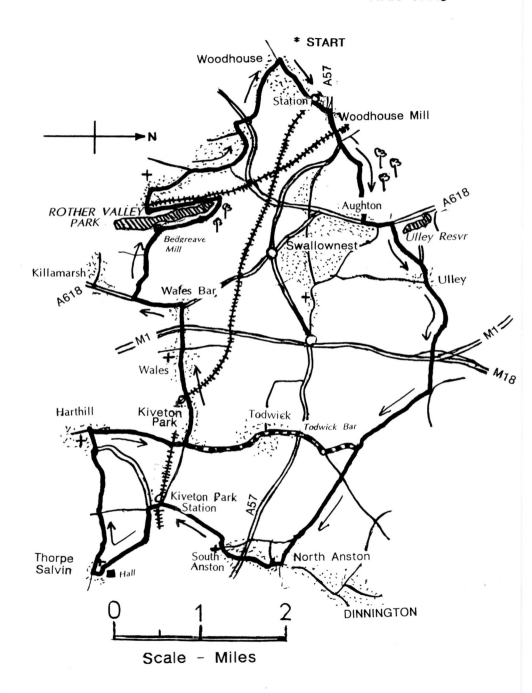

Scale - Miles

0   1   2

WOODHOUSE, N. & S. ANSTON, THORPE SALVIN, KIVETON PARK and ROTHER VALLEY

"A Tudor Hall, a Canal and a Ride Through the Park"

Start: Woodhouse Railway Station, Furnace Lane or alternatively Ulley Country Park on the A618 Rotherham – Mansfield Road.
Car Parking: Alongside Railway Station or Ulley Country Park.
Maps: OS Landranger 111, OS Pathfinder 744.

The route weaves its way along backways and country lanes largely avoiding built up areas. It provides an opportunity to explore the quiet countryside in the southern corner of the county with an optional diversion to Thorpe Salvin near to the boundary with Nottinghamshire. One of the highlights of the ride is a visit to the Rother Valley Country Park, a recreational area catering for water sports. This is left by following a cycling route around the Park lakes to the exit to Beighton.

GRADIENTS:
After climbing from Woodhouse Mill to Aughton and another short climb to Ulley, the terrain is very gentle and does not present any problem.

Miles	Places and Route Itinerary	Information and Points of Interest
0	**WOODHOUSE** Descend Furnace Lane to the T-junction with the A57 at:	An outer suburb of Sheffield. Railway station and shops.
0.5	**WOODHOUSE MILL** Turn right (dual carriageway), cross the railway bridge and immediately turn left (Falconer Lane) then turn right (Smallage Lane); climb a narrow byroad, steeply at times, then continue to:	River Rother. Shops.
1.5	**AUGHTON** At the T-junction (A618), turn left and after a short descent at the cross-roads, turn right (signposted Ulley); descend into valley alongside Ulley Reservoir and then climb steeply into:	An unspectacular village on B6053. Shops. Ulley Country Park on the left.

Miles	Places and Route Itinerary	Information and Points of Interest
1.5	**ULLEY** Continue ahead through the village and pass under bridges (M1 and M18 junction); at the staggered cross-roads turn right; (see note (a) below); in two miles at cross-roads (B6463), continue straight ahead; in one and a half miles fork left and climb steeply; pass through stoops into:	A small hilltop village with a public house.
1.5	**NORTH ANSTON** Turn right (B6060 Nursery Road) and descend then climb to traffic lights (A57); continue ahead and climb into:	A large village closely linked to Dinnington. Shops.
1	**SOUTH ANSTON** At the T-junction turn right then fork left (High Street); at the T-junction (B6059) turn left and after a short climb continue into open country then descend to:	A small village bypassed by A57.
1	**KIVETON PARK STATION** At the foot of the hill, turn left across a level crossing; climb to cross-roads (see note (b) below) and turn left; continue to:	A railway station and close by the Chesterfield Canal.
1.5	**THORPE SALVIN** At the T-junction turn right and climb past the church; continue into open country; at cross-roads continue straight ahead to:	One of South Yorkshire's most pleasant corners with a ruined Tudor Hall (not open) and an interesting church. Public house.
2	**HARTHILL** At the T-junction turn right; cross the railway bridge and climb to cross-roads; turn left through:	Centre of village to left. Shops. There is an old mounting block, and a plaque recording the history of the village. It was mentioned by Walter Scott in "Ivanhoe".
2	**KIVETON PARK** Continue through village to:	A former colliery village with shops and a railway station.
1	**WALES** Continue ahead and cross the bridge (M1); descend to cross-roads at:	Shops and an ancient church with a Norman archway.
0.5	**WALES BAR** Turn left (A618) and after a short descent turn right into:	Shops.

Miles	Places and Route Itinerary	Information and Points of Interest
2	**ROTHER VALLEY PARK** Follow the drive around the lakes (gated) and in two miles leave by the exit on the far side of the lakes passing through a chicane barrier and under the railway bridge; and at traffic island continue ahead then fork left on the Cycle Way; at the T-junction turn right on signed Cycle Way; and at the end of this continue along School Road into:	The Park project was launched in 1970 on a former derelict site, the River Rother being diverted to form lakes. The track around the lakes is unsurfaced but quite rideable. Cafe and Cycle hire, water sports and Bedgrave Mill.
2.5	**BEIGHTON** At the T-junction turn right (High Street); at the foot of the hill fork left (Woodhouse Lane); continue to traffic island (Moss Way); continue ahead and climb up Beighton Road into:	A former Derbyshire village now an outer suburb of Sheffield. Shops. Take care at traffic island when crossing Moss Way.
1	**WOODHOUSE** To return to starting point at Railway Station, turn right (Station Road).	Centre of village to left. Shops. A former West Riding village now a suburb of Sheffield. End.

NOTES:
(a) The ride may be shortened by turning right and riding direct to Kiveton Park via Todwick.
(b) The ride may be shortened by two miles by turning right at the cross-roads shortly after Kiveton Park Station and riding direct to Harthill. This omits Thorpe Salvin.

The ruined Tudor Hall at Thorpe Salvin (Ride 9)

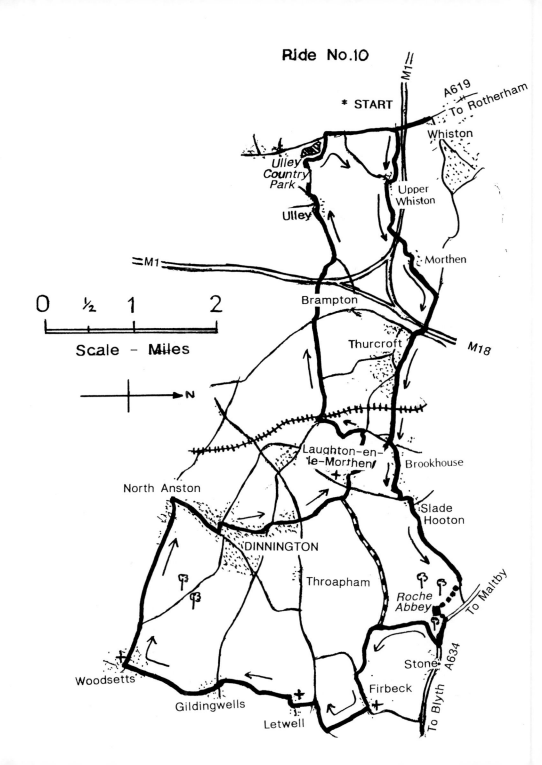

WHISTON, THURCROFT, FIRBECK, DINNINGTON and LAUGHTON

"Sleepy Villages, a Beautiful Abbey and a Mighty Spire"

Start: Whiston Village, off A616 two miles east of Rotherham.
Car Parking: Ulley Country Park, one and a half miles south.
Maps: OS Landranger 111, OS Pathfinder 744.

This ride is through the wedge of open country between the A631 and the A57. For the most part, the route follows quiet country byroads with less than one mile along main roads. It provides an opportunity to visit the ruins of Roche Abbey in a delightful wooded valley and to explore quiet villages such as Upper Whiston, Morthen, Brookhouses, Slade Hooton, Firbeck, Letwell and Ulley. Like the previous route, motorways are never far away but they are usually out of sight and the roar of traffic is quickly left behind.

GRADIENTS:
There are a few short climbs but none of them too strenuous.

Miles	Places and Route Itinerary	Information and Points of Interest
0	**WHISTON** Follow the A618 south and climb to the bridge (M1); immediately turn left (signposted Morthen) on byroad to:	An ancient thatched tithe barn, shops and public house.
1.5	**UPPER WHISTON** Turn left and again cross the M1; continue ahead through:	Although so close to M1, it is a quiet farming village.
1	**MORTHEN** At the T-junction turn right; and then continue ahead (B6060), cross the bridge (M1) into:	Another quiet farming village with a craft centre.
1.5	**THURCROFT** Continue ahead and when the B6060 turns right, fork left (Sandy Lane); at the next junction fork left (Seadfolds Lane); descend to the T-junction and turn left through:	A former colliery village. Shops. Cycle shop.
1	**BROOKHOUSE** Continue through the village and climb to the T-junction; turn left and climb to:	A picturesque village with a stream flowing by its cottages. Public house.

Miles	Places and Route Itinerary	Information and Points of Interest
1	**SLADE HOOTON** Fork right (signposted Roche Abbey) on a narrow byroad; pass under the railway bridge then continue through open country; descend and at the foot of the hill turn right on an unsurfaced drive to:	A picturesque small village on the slopes of the valley.
1.5	**ROCHE ABBEY** Return to the gate and turn sharp right; climb up cobbled drive then continue on surfaced road to the T-junction (A634); turn right and in a half mile at the outskirts of:	The Abbey ruins, built c.1187, are in a picturesque setting in a wooded valley. It is an English Heritage site open daily 10-6 in the summer.
1	**STONE** Turn right on a narrow byroad (no signpost) and climb for a half mile then continue to the T-junction (see note (a) below); turn left and descend into:	The Estate Village for Sandbeck Hall.
2	**FIRBECK** Turn right opposite the church and climb to the T-junction (B6463); turn right and in 400 yds turn left on a byroad to:	A quiet village with a modern church.
1.5	**LETWELL** Turn right then left; continue to cross-roads at:	Picturesque cottages and a church in cul-de-sac to the right.
1	**GILDINGWELLS** Continue straight ahead to:	A small farming village.
1.5	**WOODSETTS** At the cross-roads turn right; in a half mile fork left and climb for one mile; continue to:	A small village with some expanding modern housing.
2	**NORTH ANSTON** At the cross-roads (B6060) turn right (Nursery Road); in one mile turn left (New Road) then turn right (Laughton Road) into:	A large village adjoining Dinnington. Shops.
2	**DINNINGTON** Continue ahead and after left-hand bend, turn right (Brecks Lane); at the staggered cross-roads continue ahead to:	A former colliery village with public houses, shops and the Pear Tree Pottery. Cafe.

Miles	Places and Route Itinerary	Information and Points of Interest
3	**LAUGHTON-en-le-MORTHEN** Continue through the village and after a short descent, turn left on byroad; in one mile at the T-junction turn right; cross the railway bridge and then fork left on a byroad; continue to the cross-roads and continue straight ahead; pass under bridges (M1 and M18) and then continue to:	A small hilltop village whose church has a prominent spire, visible over a wide area. Close by is the site of a castle.
4	**ULLEY** Continue through the village and fork right; descend to the Reservoir and continue to the T-junction (A618); turn right and after a short climb continue ahead then cross the bridge (M1); descend to:	A small hilltop village with a public house. Ulley Country Park is on the left.
2.5	**WHISTON**	End.

NOTE:

(a) The ride may be shortened by turning right at the top of the climb after Stone and riding direct to Laughton-en-le-Morthen.

The Norman ruins of Roche Abbey, near Maltby (Ride 10)

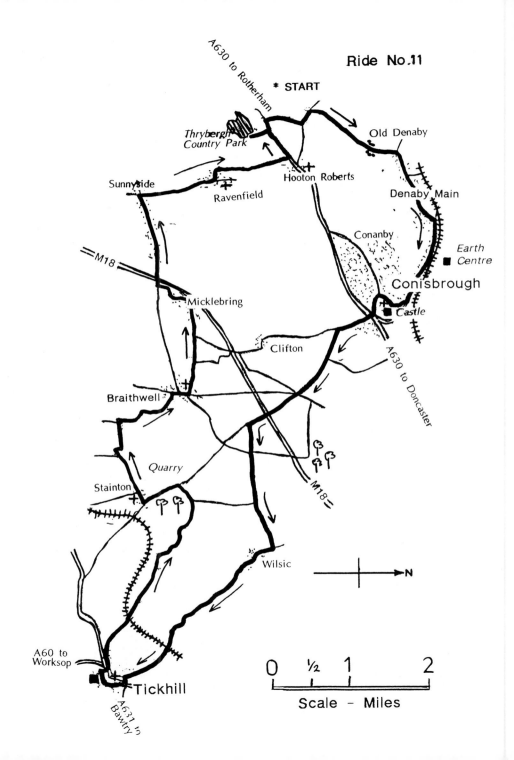

Ride No.11

THRYBERGH, DENABY, CONISBROUGH, TICKHILL and BRAITHWELL

"A Country Park, Ivanhoe's Castle and the Earth Centre"

Start: Thrybergh Country Park, on A630, three miles north east of Rotherham.
Car Parking: Thrybergh Country Park.
Maps: OS Landranger 111, OS Pathfinder 727.

Although the area to the north east of Rotherham is criss-crossed by motorways and busy main roads, it is possible to search out quiet byways ideal for leisurely cycling. From Thrybergh Country Park this route follows a byroad through old Denaby to Denaby Main and then continues to Conisbrough where the main attraction is the castle. There are then more byways through open countryside to Tickhill close to the boundary with Nottinghamshire. The return is through the sleepy villages of Micklebring, Braithwell and Ravenfield.

GRADIENTS:
Apart from a short climb into Conisbrough and another on leaving, this is a relatively easy ride.

Miles	Places and Route Itinerary	Information and Points of Interest
0	**THRYBERGH Country Park** At the exit, turn left (A630) and in 100 yds turn right into a byroad (Carr Lane); continue to the T-junction (B6090); turn left and in 400 yds turn right (opposite a white cottage); continue on a byroad through:	A former Reservoir in a pleasant situation with much wildlife. Take care when turning from the A630 into Carr Lane. There are fine views across the Don Valley to Mexborough and the hills beyond.
2.5	**OLD DENABY** Continue ahead and after a short climb descend to the T-junction (A6023); turn right through:	A mixture of old and new houses. Ferry Lane on left once led to a ferry across the River Don and canal, now replaced by a footbridge which gives access to Mexborough.
1.5	**DENABY MAIN** Continue ahead and in a half mile turn left across the railway bridge to:	A former colliery village. Shops.
0.5	**EARTH CENTRE** Return route to main road and turn left; pass the railway station and immediately turn right at the Railway Inn; climb into:	Opened in July 1995, a visit to the Earth Centre is recommended for anyone interested in the conservation of the countryside. Open daily, admission charge. There is a Cycle Trail in the grounds.

Miles	Places and Route Itinerary	Information and Points of Interest
0.5	**CONISBROUGH** At the top of the hill turn right to the gate of the Castle; on leaving turn left and descend to the T-junction (A6023); turn right and at the staggered cross-roads (junction A630) turn right and immediately turn left (B6094 Clifton Hill); climb and then continue past the Golf Course; climb to a road junction at Edlington cross-roads and continue straight ahead; cross the bridge (M18) then turn left (B6094); in one and a/ half miles at the T-junction turn right through:	The Castle, with its impressive Norman keep, was built in c.1180 and was the inspiration for "Rotherwood" in Sir Walter Scott's novel "Ivanhoe". There is an interesting Visitor's Centre in a building resembling a jousting tent. St. Peter's Church is also interesting. Shops. Early closing Thursday. Market Day Friday. Cafe.
4.5	**WILSIC** Continue on byroad through open country to outskirts of:	A hamlet whose Hall is now a school.
2.5	**TICKHILL** Turn left (Maugham Lane) and at the T-junction turn right along the main street (A60); continue ahead and at right hand bend fork left to the Dam; fork right along Dam Road; at the T-junction (A60) turn left and then right (Rawson Road); at the T-junction turn left (Pinfold Lane); continue ahead along a narrow byroad through open fields; in three miles at the T-junction turn left; continue to the T-junction at entrance to a quarry; turn left to:	An ancient and once important market town with ancient houses. The Butter Cross was built c.1779. St. Mary's Church was built c.1340 and there is a castle mound (no access to public). Cafe.
3.5	**STAINTON** At the church, turn right then fork right then left; continue past the quarry; in one mile at the T-junction turn right to:	The area has been spoiled by extensive quarrying but vehicles are directed away from the village. The 16th century church has a Norman font.
3	**BRAITHWELL** At the cross-roads turn right through the centre of the village then turn left (signposted Micklebring); continue past the church into open country; continue to:	A quiet village with a pump. Shops.
1.5	**MICKLEBRING** Turn left through the village and continue to the T-junction; turn right across the bridge (M18) and continue to the cross-roads at:	A small village close to the M18 but not spoiled by it.

Miles	Places and Route Itinerary	Information and Points of Interest
2	**SUNNYSIDE** Turn right (B6093) and descend into:	
1.5	**RAVENFIELD** Continue ahead and descend to the T-junction (A630); turn left and in a half-mile turn left to:	A small village of stone cottages and some modern housing. The church is in a cul-de-sac to the right. The village of Hooton Roberts is to the right.
1.5	**THRYBERGH Country Park**	End.

The Butter Cross and village pump at Tickhill (Ride 11)

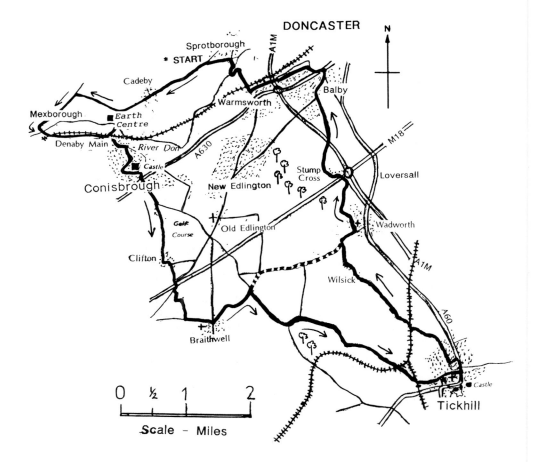

DONCASTER

N

Sprotborough

* START

Cadeby

Mexborough

Earth
Centre

Denaby Main

River Don

A630

Warmsworth

Balby

M18

Conisbrough

Castle

New Edlington

Stump
Cross

Loversall

Golf
Course

Old Edlington

Wadworth

A1M

Clifton

Wilsick

A60

Braithwell

Tickhill

Castle

0   ½   1   2

Scale - Miles

Ride No. 12   25.5 Miles

SPROTBOROUGH, MEXBOROUGH, CONISBROUGH, TICKHILL and WADWORTH

"A Canal, Two Castles and a Nature Reserve"

Start: Sprotborough Bridge, 3 miles west of Doncaster.
Alternative starting points: Balby or Denaby Ings.
Car Parking: Sprotborough side of the canal.
Maps: OS Landranger 111, OS Pathfinder 716 & 727.

The first part of this ride provides for visits to the Denaby Ings Nature Reserve, the Earth Centre at Denaby Main and Conisbrough Castle. On the return the route climbs to open country and then follows quiet byroads to the outskirts of Doncaster. At Balby the route is somewhat complicated as it passes through a residential housing estate to avoid the heavy traffic along the A630 and the A1M junction. Part of the route around Tickhill overlaps Ride No. 11 although this diversion may be omitted by riding direct from Clifton to the Wilsic junction.

GRADIENTS:

It is not a strenuous ride. There is a climb on leaving Sprotborough Bridge, a short climb to Conisbrough Castle and further climbs on leaving Conisbrough and through Clifton. There is a steep descent with some sharp bends on returning to Sprotborough Bridge.

Miles	Places and Route Itinerary	Information and Points of Interest
0	**SPROTBOROUGH BRIDGE** Take Nursery Lane alongside the canal and pass the Boat Inn; climb through woods to the T-junction; turn left and climb into open country; continue to:	Sprotborough Village (half-mile north) is now virtually a suburb of Doncaster, and is a mixture of old and new. It is in a picturesque situation above the River Don and the South Yorkshire Navigation Canal. The church is 13th century and has many ancient and curious contents.
1.5	**CADEBY** Continue through village and after a steep descent, continue to:	A peaceful village on the back road from Mexborough to Doncaster.
1.5	**DEARNE BRIDGE** At the T-junction turn left across the bridge and past Car Park (on left); continue to the outskirts of:	Denaby Ings Nature Reserve is on the left.
1.0	**MEXBOROUGH** Turn left (A6073) and cross bridges (Canal and River Don) and then the level crossing; continue through:	Shops.

Miles	Places and Route Itinerary	Information and Points of Interest
1.0	**DENABY MAIN** Turn left across railway bridge to:	A former colliery village. Shops.
0.5	**EARTH CENTRE** Return to the main road and turn left; continue past Conisbrough Station; immediately turn right and climb into:	Opened in July 1995, a visit to the Earth Centre is recommended for anyone interested in the conservation of the countryside. Open daily – admission charges. There is a Cycle Trail in the grounds.
1.0	**CONISBROUGH** At top of hill turn right to gate to Castle; on leaving turn left and descend steeply to T-junction (A6023); turn right; continue to staggered cross-roads (junction A630); turn right and immediately turn left (B6094 Clifton Hill); climb steeply and then fork right; after descent climb steeply through:	The Castle, with its impressive Norman keep was built c.1180 and was the inspiration for "Rotherwood" in Sir Walter Scott's novel "Ivanhoe". There is an interesting Visitor's Centre in a building resembling a jousting tent. St. Peter's Church is also interesting. Shops. Early closing Thursday. Market Day Friday. Cafe.
1.5	**CLIFTON** Turn left and in a half-mile continue straight ahead; at the T-junction turn right; cross the bridge (M18) and immediately turn left on a narrow byroad; in a half-mile at the T-junction turn left into:	Although near to a motorway, the small village is 'hidden' along a quiet byroad.
2.0	**BRAITHWELL** At the cross-roads fork left on a byroad (Cockhill Field Lane); in a half-mile at the cross-roads turn right (see note (a) below); in one mile turn left (Lime Kiln Lane) and in a half-mile turn right on narrow byroad (no signpost); continue through open fields to:	A large village of farms and cottages with an ancient cross, a village pump and an interesting church. Shops.
4.5	**TICKHILL** Turn left past the church and then turn right on a narrow street to the T-junction; turn left and in a half-mile turn left (Maugham Lane, signposted Car Park); at the T-junction turn right (Wilsic Road); after a left hand bend turn right (Wilsic Lane); continue through open country to:	An ancient and once important market town with some old houses. The Butter Cross was built c.1779. St. Mary's Church was built c.1340 and there is a Castle Mound (no access to public).
2.5	**WILSIC** At T-junction (B6064), fork right and continue to:	A hamlet whose Hall is now a schol.

Miles	Places and Route Itinerary	Information and Points of Interest
1.0	**WADWORTH** Turn left (Wadworth Hall Lane) past the church and continue on a byroad; descend and at the T-junction turn left under the bridge (M18 and A1M junction); climb past:	A pleasant village of stone cottages with an impressive church. Although on the A60 Doncaster-Tickhill road, many of the cottages are hidden away along quiet backroads which are followed by this route. Public house and shops.
1	**STUMP CROSS Farm** Continue ahead and pass under the bridge (A1M); continue along Springwell Lane and at the T-junction turn right; continue to the traffic lights (junction A630); at:	An isolated farm house looking on to a busy motorway junction.
3.0	**BALBY** Turn right and in 50 yds at the next traffic lights turn left (Oswin Avenue); turn left immediately after Balby College; climb for 200 yds then continue ahead on a narrow track; continue along St. Peter's Road then Church Lane; fork right (Tenter Lane), cross the bridge (A1M) and at the T-junction (Mill Lane) turn right; in a half-mile descend steeply (sharp bends) and cross bridges (River Don and Canal); turn left to Car Park at:	A residential suburb of Doncaster. There is usually heavy traffic on the A630. *Take care when crossing the main road.*
2.5	**SPROTBOROUGH BRIDGE**	End.

NOTE:

(a) The ride may be shortened and Tickhill omitted by continuing straight ahead and at the T-junction turning right to rejoin the main route at Wilsic junction. Total distance then 20.5 miles.

The superb Norman Keep at Conisbrough Castle (Ride 12)

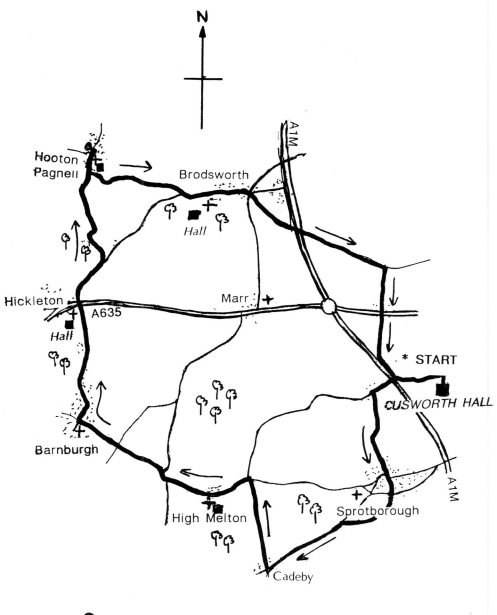

N

Hooton Pagnell

Brodsworth

A1M

Hall

Hickleton

A635

Marr

Hall

Barnburgh

* START

CUSWORTH HALL

A1M

High Melton

Sprotborough

Cadeby

0   ½   1   2

Scale - Miles

CUSWORTH, SPROTBOROUGH, BARNBURGH, HICKLETON and BRODSWORTH

"A Handful of Country Houses and a Murderous Cat!"

Start: Cusworth Hall Country Park on a byroad two miles north west of Doncaster.
Car Parking: Cusworth Hall Country Park.
Maps: OS Landranger 111, OS Pathfinder 716.

To the north west of Doncaster are some pleasant villages – High Melton, Barnburgh, Hickleton, Hooton Pagnell and Brodsworth – and quiet country byways in a small area which is free of industry. At Cusworth Hall, the starting point for this ride, is an interesting museum and cafe. From here the ride makes a circuit through open country.

GRADIENTS:
Like most routes around Doncaster, the gradients are gently undulating with just a few short climbs, e.g. from Barnburgh to Hickleton and after leaving Brodsworth. These are unlikely to present any problem.

Miles	Places and Route Itinerary	Information and Points of Interest
0	**CUSWORTH HALL** Turn left at the exit; pass under the bridge (M1) and then turn left (Spring Lane); continue to cross-roads at:	The Hall was built in the mid-18th century and is the former home of the Wrightson family, now a Museum. It has a display of vintage cycles. There are picnic places in the park and a cafe in the house.
2	**SPROTBOROUGH** At the cross-roads continue straight ahead and at the T-junction (near church) turn right then fork left (Boat Lane); descend and then fork right (Nursery Lane); climb to the T-junction and turn left (Doncaster Road); continue through open country to:	The village is now virtually a suburb of Doncaster and is a mixture of old and new. It is in a picturesque situation on a hillside above the river Don and the South Yorkshire Navigation Canal. The church is 13th century and has many ancient and curious artefacts.
1.5	**CADEBY** Turn right on a byroad and in one mile at the cross-roads turn left through:	A small village on the hillside above the Dearne Valley.
1.5	**HIGH MELTON** Descend for a half-mile ignoring all side roads; continue to:	The Hall is now a College standing in parkland. The church has an unusually long chancel, a screen and a font.
2	**BARNBURGH** In the centre of the village turn right and climb to:	A pleasant old world village with a 16th century Hall. In the church porch Sir Percival Cressacre was reputedly killed by a wild cat. The church also contains a 14th century oak tomb in the form of a grisly skeleton. Outside the village is an old pound or 'pinfold' for stray animals.

Miles	Places and Route Itinerary	Information and Points of Interest
1.5	**HICKLETON** At the crossroads continue straight ahead; in a half-mile fork left to:	Stands at the cross-roads on the A635 Barnsley to Doncaster road but we climb to it by a lesser used byroad. The Hall, formerly the seat of the Earls of Halifax, is now a Sue Ryder Home. St. Wilfred's Church contains the flag of a Dutch Admiral, interesting monuments and a lych-gate containing three human skulls.
2	**HOOTON PAGNELL** Retrace the route for 200 yds then turn left; continue through:	An attractive village of stone cottages on the edge of an escarpment giving good views. There is an interesting church with noon-day chimes and a Hall with a fine 14th century gateway.
2	**BRODSWORTH** In a half-mile fork right; pass under the bridge (M1) and climb for a half-mile; in a further half-mile turn right (signposted Cusworth); at the staggered cross-roads continue ahead; at the junction turn left and return to:	This is the old village to distinguish it from the former colliery village (one and a half miles east). The road is tree lined and it is difficult to imagine that a motorway is less than a mile away. The Victorian Hall, formerly the seat of the Thellusons, has recently been restored by English Heritage and is open to the public.
4	**CUSWORTH HALL**	End.

The lych-gate at St. Wilfred's Church, Hickleton (Ride 13)

The interesting church of St. Mary's, Sprotborough   (Ride 13)

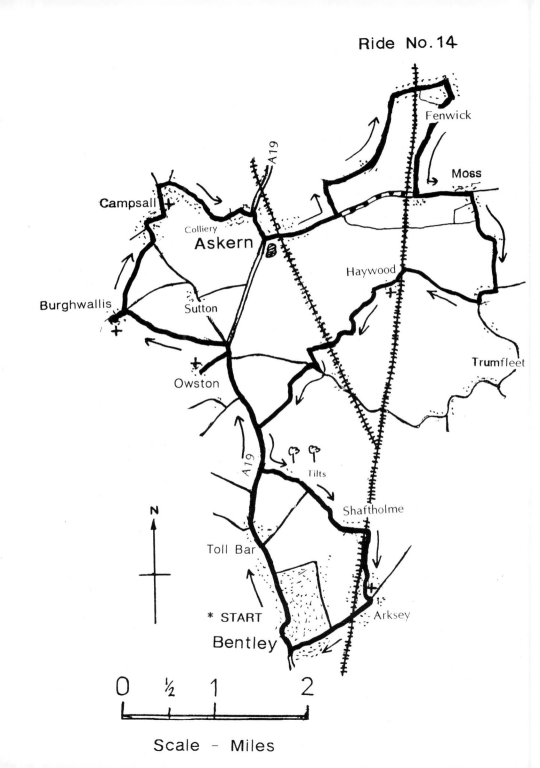

Ride No. 14

Fenwick

Moss

Campsall

Colliery

Askern

A19

Haywood

Burghwallis

Sutton

Trumfleet

Owston

A19

Tilts

Shaftholme

N

Toll Bar

* START

Arksey

Bentley

0   ½   1   2

Scale - Miles

BENTLEY, OWSTON, ASKERN, HAYWOOD and ARKSEY

"Quiet Byroads and Forgotten Villages"

Start: Bentley on the A19, two miles north of Doncaster.
Car Parking: Bentley, Old Hall Road, off High Street.
Maps: OS Landranger 111, OS Pathfinder 704 & 716.

This ride explores the countryside to the north of Doncaster. The first few miles are along the A19 Selby road but the route then turns along some quiet byroads. There is an optional diversion into the sleepy village of Owston which 'hides' in a cul-de-sac. After Campsall, the recommended route turns to Askern, once a spa but in more recent years better known for its colliery. Here there is a pleasant park in which is a cafe. After an optional diversion to the secluded village of Fenwick, the return is along a quiet and little used byroad through the tiny village of Haywood after which there is another optional diversion through Shaftholme.

GRADIENTS:
The gradients are very easy. It is unlikely that even an inexperienced rider will have to walk any hills.

Miles	Places and Route Itinerary	Information and Points of Interest
0	**BENTLEY** From the centre of the village, take the A19 north through:	A small mining town. Shops. Early closing Thursday. There is also a monument to Joseph Walker, associated with the St. John's Ambulance Brigade. Cycle shop.
1.5	**TOLL BAR** Continue ahead into open country; turn left through a gate (cul-de-sac) and into:	A straggling village on the A19 Doncaster - Selby road.
2.5	**OWSTON** Retrace the route to the junction A19; turn left and immediately turn left again on a byroad; in 250 yards again turn left and continue to the junction at outskirts of:	A beautiful secluded spot with cottages and a farm hidden amongst woods at the end of a lane. The church, with its 12th century tower, contains marble monuments by the sculptor Chantry.
2	**BURGHWALLIS** Continue straight ahead and in a mile turn left into:	A small village amongst woods, well worth a visit.

Miles	Places and Route Itinerary	Information and Points of Interest
1.5	**CAMPSALL** Continue through the village and turn right; in 200 yds again turn right and continue past Askern Country Park to the junction with the A19; turn right into:	A pleasant village of stone-built cottages and an impressive church with a fine west tower and Norman work.
2	**ASKERN** In the centre of the village turn left; continue ahead across the level crossing and in a half-mile turn left (Fenwick Lane) (see note (a); continue through open country; again cross the level crossing into:	A former spa town spoiled by coal mining, but still with a picturesque heart with a lake in a small park. Alongside the lake is a cafe which is open daily and is popular with cyclists. Shops. Early closing Wednesday and Market Day on Friday.
3.5	**FENWICK** Turn right (Fenwick Common Road) and in one and a half miles at the T-junction turn left into:	An isolated village of farms and a few cottages near to the boundary with West Yorkshire.
1.5	**MOSS** In a half-mile turn right (signposted Bramwith) and in 1.5 miles turn right to outskirts of:	A straggling village on a byroad from Askern to Sykehouse.
1.5	**TRUMFLEET** Turn right and cross the level crossing into:	Consists of a few farms overshadowed by the cooling towers of Thorpe Marsh Power Station. The railway is the main East Coast line from London to Scotland.
1.5	**HAYWOOD** Continue ahead on a winding byroad; cross the level crossing at the next junction; turn right then left; continue through:	An almost 'forgotten' village hidden away along winding country lanes, seen more by rail travellers than those in cars. The church is now in ruins but it has an impressive spire visible over a wide area.
2.5	**HOLME** Continue to the T-junction (A19); turn left and in a half-mile turn left on a byroad (no signpost) to:	Farms and cottages.
2.5	**SHAFTHOLME** Cross the level crossing and immediately turn right; continue to:	A quiet farming hamlet.
1	**ARKSEY** Turn right (High Street) and after passing the church turn right; cross the level crossing and continue into:	A quiet village with a few older cottages and some modern housing. There is a church, an old school and some almshouses.
1	**BENTLEY**	End.

NOTE:
(a) The diversion around Fenwick might be omitted and the distance shortened by riding direct from Askern to Moss.

The Church of All Saints at Hooton Pagnell   (Ride 13)

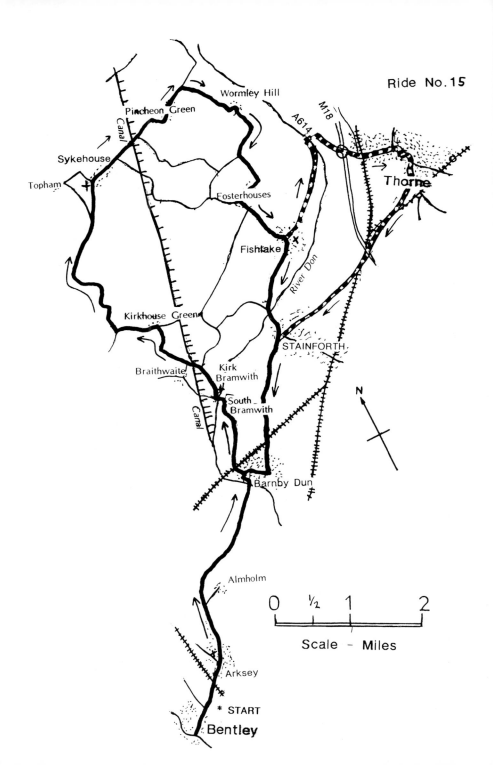

Ride No.15

Wormley Hill

Pincheon Green

M18

A614

Canal

Sykehouse

Topham

Thorne

Fosterhouses

Fishlake

River Don

Kirkhouse Green

STAINFORTH

Braithwaite

Kirk
Bramwith

South
Bramwith

Canal

N

Barnby Dun

Almholm

0   ½   1   2

Arksey

Scale - Miles

* START

Bentley

Ride No. 15   26.5 Miles

BENTLEY, BARNBY DUN, SYKEHOUSE, FISHLAKE and THORNE

"A River, Two Canals and a Ride Across the Flatlands"

Start: Bentley.
Car Parking: Bentley, Old Hall Road (signs from High Street) or Cooke Street.
Maps: OS Landranger 111, OS Pathfinder 705, 716 & 717.

This is an extension of Ride No. 14 and an experienced rider might accomplish both rides in one day. Most of the route is through open countryside and, after the village of Barnby Dun, it keeps close company with the River Don and the South Yorkshire Navigation Canal. From Fishlake, there is an optional diversion to Thorne, a small market town with several cafes and a cycle shop. Whilst the scenery may not be dramatic, the network of byways provides some excellent cycling routes.

GRADIENTS:
A very easy ride, the steepest climb being over the bridges of disused railway lines. Even the misnamed hamlet of Wormley Hill does not have a hill.

Miles	Places and Route Itinerary	Information and Points of Interest
0	**BENTLEY** In the centre of the village turn along Arksey Lane; cross the level crossing and continue along Station Road into:	A small mining town. Shops. Early closing Thursday. Cycle shop. There is a monument to Joseph Walker, associated with the St. John's Ambulance Brigade.
1	**ARKSEY** Continue ahead (Almholme Road) and in a mile fork left; continue ahead and cross the canal; turn left into:	A quiet village with a few older cottages and some modern housing. There is a church, an old school and some almshouses.
3	**BARNBY DUN** Turn left past the church; again turn left; continue across the level crossing to:	A few older houses cluster around the church but the remainder of the village is largely modern housing. The church has some interesting gargoyles. The nearby South Yorkshire Navigation Canal is crossed by a swing bridge rebuilt in recent years.
1.5	**SOUTH BRAMWITH** Turn left and cross the canal bridge to:	A hamlet of farms and cottages divided from Kirk Bramwith by the canal and the River Don.

Miles	Places and Route Itinerary	Information and Points of Interest
0.5	**KIRK BRAMWITH** Turn right past the church; again cross the canal and continue to the T-junction at:	A tiny community with an impressive 12th century church which has a fine Norman doorway and a font. There has been less development here than at other nearby villages.
1	**KIRKHOUSE GREEN** At the T-junction turn left; cross the bridge (disused railway) and continue to the T-junction; turn right on a byroad to:	A scattered hamlet at the junction of byroads to Askern, Fishlake and Kirk Bramwith. Public house.
3	**SYKEHOUSE** Continue ahead and again cross the canal to:	A rather remote village whose cottages straggle along a byroad. Opposite to the small church is a green with seats convenient for a picnic. Nearby in the garden of a bungalow is a narrow gauge railway.
1.5	**PINCHEON GREEN** After a half-mile turn right on a byroad and continue through:	A hamlet of farms and cottages.
1	**WORMLEY HILL** Continue ahead to:	A farming hamlet. Misnamed as there is no evidence of a hill within sight!
1.5	**FOSTERHOUSES** At the T-junction turn left then turn right into:	A collection of farms and cottages.
2.5	**FISHLAKE** (See note (a) below); continue through the village and cross the bridges (River Don and Canal) into:	A pleasant village of old cottages. A disused windmill and a church with a 15th century tower and carvings. Shops and a public house. There is a pinfold or pound for stray animals.
3.5	**STAINFORTH** In the centre of the village, turn right and in 200 yds again turn right then left on a byroad; continue ahead to:	Much of the older part of the village is now swallowed up by a housing estate. Shops. Early closing Wednesday. Railway station and cycle repairs.
2.5	**BARNBY DUN** At the left hand bend turn right into Church Road then turn left into Madam Road; at the cross-roads continue ahead over the canal bridge (retracing outward route); continue through:	See above.
3	**ARKSEY** To:	See above.
1	**BENTLEY**	End.

NOTE:

(a)   The ride may be extended to Thorne as follows :–

Miles	Places and Route Itinerary	Information and Points of Interest
3	**FISHLAKE** Retrace the route along Pinfold Road; at the T-junction turn right; in one and and a half miles cross the bridge (River Don) and at the T-junction (A614) turn right; at motorway junction continue straight ahead into: **THORNE** Continue through the town centre; cross the bridge (Stainforth & Keadby Canal) and immediately turn right on a byroad; continue passing under the bridge (M18) and over the level crossing to:	A small bustling town with a weekly market on Friday and Saturday. Early closing Thursday. Railway station. The main road (A614) has now bypassed the town with the construction of the M18. The canal is popular with boating people. The church has a 12th century nave. Much of the surrounding area was once the fenland of Hatfield Chase which was drained by the Dutch engineer Vermuyden in the 1630's. Cafe.
1.5	**STAINFORTH** Then continue as main route.	
	This extension increases the total mileage for the ride to 31.	

Cyclist's enjoying an off-highway route through Wharncliffe Woods (Ride 4)

OTHER CYCLING GUIDES
by
ARNOLD ROBINSON

CYCLING WORLD MAGAZINE
'Andrew House', 2a Granville Road, Sidcup, Kent DA14 4BN.

Cycling in London and the Home Counties
Cycling in the Northern Highlands

DALESMAN PUBLISHING CO. LTD.
Broughton Hall, Skipton, North Yorkshire BD23 3AE.

Cycling in the Yorkshire Dales

FOOTPRINT PRESS LTD.
19 Moseley Street, Ripley, Derbyshire DE5 3DA.

Cycling Around Buxton
Cycling Around Castleton and the Hope Valley
Cycling Around Chesterfield
Cycling Around the Cotswolds
Cycling Around the Lake District
Cycling Around Leicestershire and Rutland
Cycling Around Lincolnshire
Cycling Around Matlock
Cycling Around the North Yorkshire Moors
Cycling Around Northumberland
Cycling Around Staffordshire
Cycling Around the Yorkshire Wolds

WYE VALLEY PRESS
Thornbridge Manor, Station Road, Great Longstone,
Derbyshire DE45 1NY.

Cycling in Derbyshire (Derbyshire Heritage)
Cycling in Nottinghamshire (Nottinghamshire Heritage)
Cycling Around Ashbourne (NMD)
Cycling Around Bakewell (NMD)
Cycling Around Hartington (NMD)
Cycling Around the Peak District (NMD)